Help! My Kid Has Homework

Help! My Kid Has Homework

◆

Secrets for Busy Moms for Making Homework and Tests Easier for Their Kids

By Joan Brown

iUniverse, Inc.

New York Lincoln Shanghai

Help! My Kid Has Homework
Secrets for Busy Moms for Making Homework and Tests Easier for Their Kids

iUniverse, Inc.

For information address:
iUniverse, Inc.
2021 Pine Lake Road, Suite 100
Lincoln, NE 68512
www.iuniverse.com

ISBN: 0-595-29502-9

Contents

ACKNOWLEDGMENTS

I first want to thank my Lord, Savior, and best friend, Jesus Christ. He was there for me while I struggled with the children with homework and waited patiently for me to seek His help.

The world's best father and husband, Joseph Brown, Jr has been my encouragement and loving critic. He's been a great source of strength and my sounding board.

Celeste and Stephen, thanks for turning out to be such wonderful, respectful, God-fearing children. Without you two I would not have written this book.

To my parents Kenneth and Joyce Peterson who trained me in the way I should go and have been great examples for me to follow and train my own children.

I owe much thanks to my two editors and friends Mrs. Sylvia Halfhide and Mr. Sherman Roberson. Mrs. Halfhide with a Master's degree from Bank Street College of Education, is presently executive director of Williston Academy in Brooklyn, New York. This elementary and preschool was founded by her in 1986 and was my children's first school. Mr. Roberson is presently a second-career elementary school teacher for the city of New York, after working years in the accounting profession. He has a Bachelor's degree in commerce from North Carolina Central University and a Master's degree in education from Brooklyn College.

I would like to acknowledge my pastor and friend for the past 19 years—Dr. A.R. Bernard Sr. and Karen Bernard, his wonderful wife, of Christian Cultural Center in Brooklyn, New York. Not only has he taught me principles to live by, but most importantly everything he teaches focuses on the Father heart of God and becoming intimate with Him. Karen has loved me in a most unique way and has been supportive of me from the beginning.

Last but not least, my mentor, my teacher, my prayer partner, my friend Mrs. Cheryl Carter I owe many, many thanks. Cheryl Carter is founder of "Organize Your Life", a company that helps individuals and groups reach their maximum effectiveness and productivity. She is a member of the National Association of Professional Organizers (NAPO) and the author of the published books "Organize Your Life," "Organizing Your Home," and "Organize Your Child." Thanks for getting me started Cheryl, taking me by the hand, and being there to the very end.

BASIC OVERVIEW

1

A WORD OF ENCOURAGEMENT

Do you have school-aged children that come home daily with homework? Are you the typical busy mom working outside the home, coming home to cook dinner, supervise homework, check it when it's done, find out about tests, help your kids to study, prepare for the next school day, play referee between arguments, prepare the kids for bed, clean up the kitchen and tidy up the house? Then you know first-hand how exhausting this can be. There is even more! When they get projects and book reports it's usually the mom assisting them by taking them to the library, buying the construction paper and coaching them along. The worst part is, after you've given so much of your evening in homework, they return with the same type work the next day, forgetting all you showed them!

You might have a child that is a slow learner and is having a challenge in comprehension and expression. This can cause the child to become frustrated with school. I have been there, and found myself feeling frustrated also. I was told by my daughter's teachers that she will always struggle in school, will always need remedial help and probably will be left back a few times.

I remember so well driving home and becoming more and more upset as I approached the house knowing that I had so much to do for myself and having to deal with my daughter and her homework. The first thing I would ask,

"How much homework do we have today?" If it was more than three assignments I would start banging the pots in the kitchen and yelling at her to start the easiest one until I could get to help her.

We would be up until 10–11 pm at nights finishing homework. She wasn't allowed any TV during the week and Saturdays was time spent on books to help her learn better. She was beginning to hate school and homework while I was having less free time and becoming more of a nag.

I prayed earnestly to the Lord to help me and both my kids. He didn't sprinkle some magical dust over me but He brought resources across my path on learning styles, comprehension disorders, etc. He began bringing to my remembrance and had me look closely at how I studied effortlessly in school and made the grades.

He showed me how I could translate that to my kids on their level while having more time for myself. He showed me how to utilize free time we had while driving in the car, learning while shopping, and teaching them more independent learning.

Then I found other parents coming to me also frustrated with homework and I was able to share with them. I had college students and adults seek me out for advice on how to study for tests and write reports.

One adult who graduated with a Bachelor's degree in nursing was afraid to get her Mater's degree because she didn't think she could write. After showing her how to write a paper and how to do research, she confidently enrolled and graduated with her Master's degree in two years.

I'm extremely excited to say that using the techniques in this book my daughter graduated from eighth grade with a Presidential Award of Excellence signed by President Bill Clinton. She made the honor roll and received two music awards for band and chorus.

When she entered high school she received both academic and attitude honor rolls for both semesters. In 10th grade she received all "A"s' on her report card. In 11th grade she was inducted in the National Honor Society, the highest academic award a student can achieve in high school. She was also inducted in the Tri-M Music Honor Society.

This was accomplished without me sitting down with her every evening. On her own she applied the techniques she was taught over time and that freed me up to do other things.

This book has been written especially for those mothers who have full schedules in and outside their homes, and are frustrated, hurried and overwhelmed with their child's homework. This book is for moms who want to see their child do well academically, grasp the art of test taking and memorization, develop their child's learning style without either feeling pressured and stressed.

With the secrets given in this book when consistently applied, you can begin to see these results. These suggestions and ideas are not hard core scientific facts researched in a laboratory, but they are compiled of my own experiences, strengths, and hopes with my children and those I've tutored over the years.

It wasn't all an easy up hill climb to the top, but there were times my kids knew how to study but just didn't want to do it "mom's way". They would do poorly and then agree to do it "mom's way" the next time. To be honest, there were times I was deciding not to complete this book because my kids started to mess up.

In trying to help your children, you will have to deal with individual character differences along with their yearning for independence from parental rule and also peer pressure.

Over time, I have seen that the time spent with my children doing homework was shortened, it was more effective with longer-lasting results, more rewarding with better grades and heightened self-esteem for myself and my children. These results can be accomplished with three principles in mind:

1) *Change is a process, not an event.* Change in your child's study habits, comprehension, self-application, etc. will not be overnight, but you will begin to see gradual improvements.

2) *Balance is the key to life.* We are uniquely created in God's image and we are affected by many things around us. By understanding your child's make-up, potential stressors, learning capabilities, and need for recreation and fun, you can help to bring balance to his/her life and make school time rewarding.

3) *It costs you something to improve the quality of anything.* If you're not willing to pay the price, you won't experience the results. The time you invest now with our children will pay big dividends later.

2

YOUR CHILD'S LEARNING STYLE

It is really true that no two people/children are alike. Even if you have identical twins there may be some similarities, but basically they are different from each other. In that respect, no two children have the same exact way of learning and perceiving the world around them. As parents and overseers of our children's education, we need to recognize and enhance their different learning styles.

Cynthia Tobias in her book, *The Way They Learn,* does an excellent job in defining and analyzing the four major dominant learning styles: concrete sequential, abstract sequential, abstract random, and concrete random. As parents we have probably seen these traits in our children.

In brief, the dominant concrete sequential child applies ideas in a practical way, works well within time limits, likes routines and is detail oriented. That's the child who becomes unglued if she comes to class and the teacher changed the desks and chairs. They tend to look at things very literally.

The dominant abstract sequential child likes using logical reasoning, learns more by watching than doing, gathers data before making decisions. That's the child who takes longer to complete assignments because they want to be thorough. They tend to be quiet and appear withdrawn while their minds are fast at work analyzing what they are seeing.

The dominant abstract random child understands feelings and emotions, is friendly with everyone and does focus on themes and ideas. That's the child who has to find out how everyone's weekend went before they can settle in to their work. They let the teacher know who's hurting or who's pet died.

The dominant concrete random child thinks fast on his feet, inspires others to take action, uses insight and instinct to solve problems. That's the child that is always coming up with brilliant ideas for the class and has everyone pitching in. They enjoy helping to make the rules and are usually strong-willed.

When you can discover your child's learning style, you can encourage them with following directions, doing homework, and studying for tests.

In trying to explain homework assignments to my son in the past, I would always insist he sit still at the table and listen to my instructions. I became frustrated because he would be fidgeting, getting up and bouncing a ball, or jumping. I would be so sure he hadn't heard a word but he would repeat everything I said correctly.

When I forced him to sit still, he hardly remembered what I said. He was probably thinking about when he would get a break to move instead of what I was teaching. I had an eye opener when I learned how to identify and work with auditory learners, visual learners, and kinesthetic learners.

Now as I go over homework with him, I try and explain challenging topics with action words, acting out, and developing acronyms to help him remember. This has been very successful.

There was one time I remember when the teacher sent home a note stating the class is having difficulty learning a concept and there will be extra time given after school. I worked with my child at home and he learned the concept quickly using motion and visualization and went back and taught the class the silly way he learned it. Extra time after school was canceled.

In addition to knowing individual learning styles, you should also incorporate your child's best methods of concentration, listening and remembering. I spent good money for a matching desk set for my child's room. It finally dawned on me that homework was completed a lot faster when my child stretched out across the bed with all the books rather than sitting at my expensive student table. I had to stop and look at the bottom line: "I wanted the homework done at a reasonable time."

Knowing your child's learning style is important, but equally important is knowing their personalities and temperaments. This helps to explain why they do what they do and how best to train them in the direction you want them to go.

You can usually identify your child's temperament at a very early age before formal education begins. Knowing in advance their temperament gives you a good idea how to relate to them and best help them in school work.

Nearly all psychologists agree that we are made up of a blend of temperaments with one or two dominant traits. In understanding the basic temperaments you'll be able to identify your child and also identify yourself and significant others. You'll even see why you do certain things the way you do and how it can enhance or irritate others.

3

THE POWER OF
MOTIVATION

Some children seem to be motivated to learn early in life. They are explorative and find learning fun. As they get older they sometimes lose their motivation for learning in spite of our showing an interest in their studies. As parents, we need to know our children individually and help them keep that motivation going. Our techniques and tactics will change as they mature and will also differ for each child. To be able to help motivate your child, you need to know your child-their likes, dislikes, interests, hobbies, etc. Tangible techniques of motivation also come in various levels or degrees.

Have you ever noticed when you tell your child to clean up his room and then he can play, it takes him all of the morning and half of the afternoon! Now with the same child and the same messy room you tell him to clean the room in one hour and he can go with you to the mall and you'll stop in the video store, you'll see not only how fast it's accomplished, but how well it's done. They really know how you like to see their room looking and with that motivation they'll give you just what they know you want. A friend of mine had labeled her child as lazy. She did everything to help him learn and finish his homework at a decent hour. Because he loved TV she allowed him to watch 1 ½ hours of TV in the evening only if his homework was done by a certain time and not 5 minutes over. He began doing it so regularly that it became a habit and after awhile he still accomplished the homework on time and didn't even watch TV.

Some children need to begin with external motivation and over time it works its way into internal motivation—they are now desiring to do well for themselves. One school of thought is never to provide any rewards for children to do what they should automatically be doing anyway. I personally believe it's how you view it. If I view it as a reward leading to a response and if I stop the reward I stop the response, then I must keep it up forever. I choose to view it as not a reward but a motivator. As I motivate by child, he/she responds positively. I continue with the motivation until the response becomes a habit. After twenty-one days a repeated consistent action becomes a habit—whether good or bad. This habit now also inadvertently produces two things: a) It creates self-motivation by building the child's self-esteem and breaking the thoughts he was developing that he couldn' t accomplish certain tasks. b) It allows his teachers to look at him in a different light as they see him excelling in areas he was once having difficulties. At that point the external motivation is no longer needed.

You need to be aware of defining first whether your child is capable of the work at that time, or he might need professional help. Motivation doesn't always have to be material things. Giving your approval or expressing how proud you are to a child is a great motivator. Letting your children overhear you brag on them and their achievements causes them to be motivated to do better. Displaying their A and B work on a bulletin board at home in an obvious place for company to see is another motivator. This way as friends pass by you can have a chance to brag on your child. You should keep in mind that bragging on a successful grade is not enough, but acknowledging effort is vitally as important. What you convey is that the intrinsic act of learning is seen as valuable to you.

It is human nature for all of us to seek approval from those we care about the most. Many parents withhold showing genuine approval for efforts done by their children because they are too busy pointing out their faults and shortcomings. When they take a look back in their past, they realize they sought the praise of their parents (many times from their fathers) and didn't get it. The very thing they said they would never do if they had children is the very same thing they find themselves doing. If that is you, then repent of this, ask God to forgive you, ask your child to forgive you and then start doing what is right. Admitting to your child that you've made an error in judgment is not a sign of weakness, but strength. Keep in mind, it takes creativity to match the level of motivation to the task you want accomplished without causing undue stress in your child.

4

STRESS IN CHILDREN

Parents need to be aware that children as well as adults are affected physically and emotionally by stress. A child under stress would not be able to comprehend and retain school work well and would find homework very tiresome. Being pressured to perform in school academically or physically, being teased or threatened by other classmates, or even just trying to be accepted in a new class can be a great source of stress for a child. As a parent you need to keep this in mind so you can better help your child deal with these stressors or if possible avoid them. Waiting to change residence until the end of the school year is better and less stressful than if you moved in mid semester. If there is stress and tension at home from a rocky marriage or an unhealthy dysfunctional living arrangement, expect it to affect the performance level of your child. It is a basic premise that a child should feel loved and accepted and be free from emotional and physical trauma in order to focus on learning in school. Having a troubled home life will distract their attention by worrying about or reflecting on personal problems.

If your child seems always to be complaining of sickness, especially stomach pains on school days, but is fine on weekends, this could be a sign of school phobia and should be discussed with your health care provider. You need to ask your child if something or someone in school is making them uncomfortable or making them feel inadequate. For a smaller child just ask them, "Do you like school? Why or Why not." They're usually pretty honest to let you know. Also observe for chronic, excessive nailbiting, becoming introverted, and other nervous behaviors and acting out. By knowing your own child and their capabilities you can eliminate the stress of performance by letting them know you are most interested in the fact that they tried and put out effort in their classwork rather than their obtaining an "A". My son used to hide his poor grades from me and only showed me his good grades. I would discover them deep in his book bag crushed up. Though I told him to bring all work home to be seen, it wasn't being done. He became compliant finally when I explained that a poor grade is only an indicator that you don't fully understand the material being taught and you need help. I told him to bring home the poor classwork papers right away so that I can help him by 'home schooling' him. Now he comes home without acting stressful and says, "Mom I need home schooling tonight on math, I got a D in class." I then use the same principles in this book to teach him, and to see the smile on his face when he gets it is priceless.

Children can produce stress upon themselves by managing their time poorly and procrastinating. Some ways to reduce self-induced stress at school is:

- Be in class on time and be prepared.

- Know the due date of all tests, assignments, reports.

- Set up a schedule, charting your progress in completing assignments.

- Don't procrastinate. Procrastination is a thief and a robber. Get to work!

Some stress is unavoidable, like the death of a family member or close friend. If you see that your child is visibly upset by the loss, do inform his/her teacher so that the teacher can be sensitive to the needs of your child and help him/her through this stressful time.

Some children experience stress from a crowded daily schedule with many activities. Many children that are sports minded find themselves engaged in two to three sporting events in a season with practice three to four times a week and competition games two to three times weekly. There are parents who don't know how to say no to their children and are also stressed out acting as chauffeurs dropping off and picking up kids for practices and games. Some parents do bring this on themselves. They want to live their lives through their children and schedule them for too many structured activities (i.e. dance classes, music classes, football team, soft ball team, tennis, acting lessons). Children need time to be creative. Children need structure, however, too much of the wrong kind of structure stifles creativity. If we continue to organize every minute of their lives they will find it difficult to organize themselves.

Another obvious stressor is your child staying up late at nights and then having to wake up early for school. At school their bodies are still tired and they tend to process information very slowly. You know what it's like as an adult not getting enough sleep and trying to stay alert behind the wheel getting to work and hoping the demands on you at work won't be much because you're not at your sharpest. When people react negatively to physical or emotional stress their metabolic rate speeds up and more nutrients are needed by the body. Therefore, when faced with stress it is important to have your child eat nutritiously in order to replace the vitamins and minerals burned up and get sufficient rest and sleep.

5

NUTRITION AND MEMORY

Having a good memory is vital in doing well in school. We as parents first need to set a good example for our children because they tend to repeat and believe what they hear us say. Let's be honest, don't you catch yourself saying things like: "I have a terrible memory.", "I'm bad with remembering names.", "I know I'll forget this.", "You're your father's son, he forgets everything also." In truth, there is usually nothing wrong with our memory but it's that we are selective in what we chose to remember because of the value we place on it.

A secret to memory is attention. If you're not paying attention when something goes by that you should be remembering you will not retain it no matter how good your memory is. If you place no value on the information, then you won't pay attention to it, therefore you won't retain it. It's like shopping, if you don't value an item, you won't pay money for it and thereby won't retain it. When you re-program yourself today by making positive statements about your own memory, you'll recognize the same in your children and soon they too will be saying "I have a good memory, I just wasn't paying attention at the time." "Now I will pay attention and I will remember the material." Your attitude determines your approach, and your approach determines your success or failure.

There are some nutritional supplements that are good for aiding memory. Below is a list of some of these supplements and some foods that contain them. Contact your physician or nutritionist for further information.

1) B-Complex Vitamins

- Vitamin B1 sources in some foods are: liver, peanuts, soybeans, brown rice lentils, corn, egg yolk.

- Vitamin B12 sources in some foods are: liver, eggs, sardines, salmon, Swiss cheese, red snapper.

- Vitamin B6 sources in some foods are: whole wheat, brown rice, tuna, bran, rye, brewer's yeast.

2) Vitamin C

- Foods with the highest amount of vitamin C are rose hip, acerola cherries, parsley, green peppers, strawberries, oranges, grapefruits.

3) Choline, a nutrient in lecithin

- Highest amounts of choline is found in soy lecithin, egg yolk, chick peas, green beans, liver, brown rice.

4) Magnesium

- Food sources for magnesium are: black strap molasses, wheat germ, sunflower seeds, almonds, kelp.

As you can see, sources of nutrients that help with memory are found in foods we eat daily. That's why it's important for your children to eat a well-balanced diet daily that includes all the food groups. I strongly recommend children also taking a daily dose of children's multivitamin tablet, along with vitamin C tablets for added protection against the common cold. The basic ingredients in most children's multivitamins contain vitamin C, vitamin E, vitamin B1 (thiamin), vitamin B12, vitamin B6 that are shown to help with memory.

Some things that need to be avoided to ensure optimal thinking are: heavy eating before mental work, eating processed foods, refined sugar and flour, excessive caffeine, and stress. Stress is definitely counterproductive to optimal thinking and overall learning. Caffeine is a drug that activates the sympathetic nervous system. This drug makes a child more jumpy. anxious, and fearful and thus can interfere with relaxation, rest, and sleep. Many parents aren't aware of the amount and effects of caffeine in foods their children eat regularly. Caffeinated beverages children usually ingest include hot tea, iced tea, hot cocoa, Coke, Pepsi, and other caffeinated sodas. Cola nuts are a stimulant and a source of caffeine. Very little cola nut goes into cola drinks but they obtain added caffeine from other sources. Chocolate contains only a small amount of caffeine but has a lot of theobromine, a close relative of caffeine with similar effects on the body. Researchers have found that chocolate can be a mood-altering substance, can affect the body and the mind and can be addictive. Pure cocoa powder found in some hot chocolates is low in fat but high in chocolate flavor. Chocolate, coffee, teas, chocolate drinks and sodas with caffeine should be limited in your child's diet.

6

COMPREHENSION DISORDER

Some children have been labeled as lazy, lacking motivation, having an attitude problem, quiet, air-heads, and even MBD (minimal brain damaged) and ADD (attention deficit disorder), when their problem was really comprehension disorder. Different disorders can be with written or oral language expression, oral language comprehension, or reading comprehension. Some of the visible symptoms are difficulty following directions, poor logical thinking, day dreaming in class, poor and slow reading ability, and seeming to miss the main idea when reading. You might even have a child that reads well with few decoding errors but has difficulty remembering the content of the material. The child may be able to decode a word/s but if he does not know what it means, the content of the material may not make sense, therefore comprehension is poor. Building vocabulary helps in some cases. Parents can build vocabulary by simply using vocabulary with their children, <u>at an early age</u>, that they would normally use when speaking with an adult. Also, a child who speaks well, with an extensive vocabulary usually becomes a good writer.

If a child has weak comprehension, poor concentration, easily distracted, poor use of or understanding the vocabulary he/she can find classwork frustrating and doesn't know why. If placed in a remedial class the emphasis is just on reading and answering questions and not on teaching <u>how to comprehend.</u> When you ask the teacher how can you help your child, you're usually told: "Sign him/her in remedial reading class and have them read a lot at home." This is a start, but they can't really answer, "How can I help my child to comprehend?" A child with a reading comprehension disorder cannot be corrected by just reading more material and answering questions. Reading and answering questions only test if the child comprehends, it doesn't teach a child how to comprehend.

Many researchers in the area of cognitive psychology and reading supports IMAGERY as a critical factor in language and reading comprehension. Very simply put, in order for the brain to remember and understand thoughts, it needs mental images. If a child can actually visualize what he's reading as he goes along, he will be better able to comprehend the main idea, conclusion, prediction, etc. Even in giving a child directions, he/she needs to visualize what task they need to carry out before saying o.k. and leaving. I used to have this problem with my children until I discovered visualization. Visualization is seeing in your mind the picture of a word or words with all the fine details including color, size, number, background, mood, etc. When I first began I asked my daughter, "When I say clown what do you see?" Her response was, "A clown." Now she responds, "I see a tall skinny man with red curly hair, large red nose, big blue eyes, white chalky face wearing red and white polka dot outfit with large black shoes and a big smile with large white teeth." After I taught them how to visualize I would tell them a ridiculous task involving eight to nine steps and they would not only repeat it correctly, but weeks later would remember it.

A more in depth source on visualization and verbalization and the method of teaching it to your child is done by Nanci Bell in her book <u>Visualizing and Verbalizing For Language Comprehension and Thinking.</u> After teaching visualizing and verbalizing to my children, I was able to see a big difference in their comprehension, ability to follow directions, improved memory, improved reading, and definite improvement in self-esteem. Social studies homework used to take so long with reading the assignment 2–3 times trying to get understanding in order to answer the few questions. Now as they are reading I call out, "Remember to use visualizing/verbalizing, see the generals in battle!" The text is read only once and the questions answered without frustration. I have discovered that not only do children suffer from comprehension disorder, but many adults who have even completed college have this problem and don't know how to correct it.

7

THE PARENT-TEACHER CONFERENCE

Just as important and necessary as textbooks, exams, assignments, and homework, is the parent-teacher conference for your young child. This time with your child's teacher can seem intimidating for some parents and even fearful for others. Sometimes these conferences bring back negative memories when we were students ourselves. Some parents feel that teachers don't really care about the students anyway and go into these conferences with a negative attitude. There are others that feel very intimidated because they as parents lack the level of education achieved by the teacher.

As parents, we need to approach the parent-teacher conference with confidence knowing that we are ourselves both teachers and caregivers and can provide valuable information on our child's personality, strengths, and learning style. Parents are their child's first teachers from birth, and they pave the way for teachers to continue that education.

Knowing ahead of time what questions to ask the teacher that will give you valuable and tangible information to work with will help boost your confidence. You need to realize that you're not just at this conference to hear how your child is getting on in class, but you're also there to share information about what you know and observe about your child that can be helpful to the teacher. Most parents sit down and ask, "So how's my child doing in class?" With that they usually leave with a short briefing of their child's overall performance and test results, and nothing shared on their part with the teacher. If you go into the conference with detailed, specific questions based on information you've learned from reading this book and being better aware of your child's strengths and weaknesses, his/her teacher will view you as a serious-minded parent concerned about your child's education.

Based on what you've learned previously in the Basic Overview on learning styles, motivation, stress in children, comprehension disorder, you can formulate questions that will provide information that will help you and the teacher work together in educating your child. I suggest you go with a written outline and a pencil to jot down the teacher's answers briefly. A suggested outline:

I. *What have you observed to be my child's learning style?*

   - *Give the teacher insight on what you've observed at home.*

II. *What are my child's academic strengths?*

III. *What are my child's personal strengths?*

   - *Share with the teacher strengths you have noticed in your child.*

IV. *What are my child's academic weaknesses?*

V. *What are my child's personal weaknesses?*

   - *Discuss how you can work with the teacher to improve one or two weaknesses by the next marking period.*

VI. *What are your expectations for my child?*

   - *Discuss how they differ or are about the same as yours.*

VII. *Discuss motivational techniques you use with your child, informing the teacher of your child's hobbies and interests.*

If you choose not to have your child present at the meeting, or if one parent could not make the conference, by addressing these questions you can thoroughly retell the content of the evaluation leaving no room for speculation. You also will now have a clear strategy on how to improve your child's performance in school and at homework time.

Homework time can be stressful for both parent and child if not structured well. Homework should be reinforcement of what should have been taught/learned in school and not an agonizing ordeal for any child and his/her parent. Some helpful secrets on studying for tests, effective memorization, being organized and much more can be valuable to help make homework easier.

SECRETS FOR DOING BETTER HOMEWORK

8

BEING ORGANIZED

An important aspect of functioning effectively academically as well as in life in general is to be organized. The Webster's dictionary defines organize as; to give a definite structure; to prepare for transaction of business; to get up, arrange, or put into working order. The more organized you and your child are, the less time you both will waste. A child can easily waste one hour looking for a pen, paper and scissors before starting homework. They become easily distracted while searching.

- If you have space in your kitchen drawer, keep a pencil case with pencil sharpener, pens, small crayon box, scissors, ruler, glue stick, liquid glue, correction fluid, paper clips, and a stapler.

- You can also store these items in a large shoebox that is easily accessible to your child, but not to be kept in their room. Somehow if it stays in their room it's soon empty and no one knows where the contents went.

- Keep a lot of scrap paper from your job that is being thrown out, outdated forms being revised, etc.

- After completing homework, they need to immediately return these items back in the box. At times you will have to check the box for missing or broken items to be replaced.

- Always have a small box of sharpened no. 2 pencils for when they have exams in school and are told to bring them in for a test.

- Keep reference books such as a dictionary, thesaurus, encyclopedia in the same spot.

- Purchase a tape recorder and blank cassette tapes, and a kitchen timer.

- A calculator is a must item, but children should not be doing their homework with it, unless the assignment specifically states so.

- Use the calculator for you or older siblings to quickly check their math homework.

- Use a kitchen timer for each assignment to allow ample time for completion.

- When it goes off, move on to the next task. If it's a long assignment this will break it up into manageable pieces. The more time given, the more time taken. Even as adults, if we have a deadline to complete a task at work, we won't even tackle it until just before the deadline. Kids are no different. Everyone likes competition and your child will use his time efficiently trying to beat the timer.

- Have a loose leaf binder notebook, or a trapper to organize papers.

- All completed homework assignments should go into one section in their binder or manila folder to hand in. It's frustrating for you to set up with your child doing homework and later find out from their teacher that it was handed in late because they couldn't find it.

In general, being organized will afford you less interruptions and less wasted time in finding items.

9

A TO-DO LIST

In keeping with being organized and focused, your child would benefit from a to-do list. This list should be made up by you for evenings after school and for weekends. This list gives them a sense of accomplishment and helps them to get back on focus when they drift. Another good benefit is it cuts down on boredom and TV watching.

- As they come home from school find out how much homework they have and in what subjects.

- Make a list, dividing their homework into parts, doing the most challenging parts first and the easiest parts last.

- Have them check off as they complete each task.

- Remember to keep your list reasonable and age appropriate.

An example of a to-do list for a ten year old boy:

- twenty minutes snack time after school

- do assigned chapter 3 in math (45 min.)

- walk the dog (25 minutes)

- read social studies and answer questions

- study for spelling test on tape

- pack bags for school and prepare clothes for the next day

- take a bath

In doing a to-do list you are teaching your child organizational skills, how to redeem the time, and how to be productive.

10

ENCOURAGING INDEPENDENCE

The purpose of applying the ideas and secrets in this book is to help your child to learn while freeing you up to do other needed things. As you work with them, encourage independence. Make use of the timers, tape recorders, study sheets, self-tests. Television can be a great tool for education as well as a reward for working independently. Limit your child's television watching time and make clear your rules and reasons. For the younger child, make up small TV and video cards from scrap paper. Have cards of 15 minutes, 30 minutes, and 1 hour. Give an hour card for completing homework independently and timely. Give a 30 minutes card if minimal help is needed from you. They can cash in their cards for TV or video viewing at appropriate times. You still monitor what they watch and whenever possible, watch programs with them. For an older child with an assignment, time him for each section and give a video card for each section completed on time. They can exchange a certain number of cards for a free video rental at the store.

As they learn to work independently, they also learn responsibility. Taking responsibility for your own actions is a sign of maturity. In essence, we are actually teaching our children how to manage in life without us and be successful at it.

11

FOLLOWING DIRECTIONS

Being able to follow directions is a very important part of learning. Some children aren't good at following directions because they have difficulty with overall comprehension, they're moving off before they hear all the directions, or some are just lacking concentration.

- First make sure you have their full attention before you give directions.

- When you ask them to do something, have them repeat it before leaving your presence.

- Have them bake a cake on their own to learn the importance of following directions.

- Make simple things as a dip, Jell-O, etc.

As your child learns how to memorize effectively, they will be better at comprehending and thereby able to follow directions. If this is a problem and you're in the process of helping them with comprehension and memorization, then make sure your child reads the directions to all assignments slowly at least twice and then tell you what he should be doing. It's frustrating for them and yourself, for example, if they have completed an English assignment to circle verbs and underline adjectives, and they circled both verbs and adjectives. This might have taken 45 minutes to do, and now it has to be erased, directions explained, and another 45 minutes to redo.

12

SOME GOLDEN NUGGETS

Here are some unrelated pieces of information in different subjects that can improve learning.

- Any text or lesson that is not easy to understand, go to the library or teacher's educational store and take out books on the same topic with a different view or explanation and different examples.

- Encourage proper speech in your children at all times. Correct their grammar as they speak. The more you hear yourself speak correctly, the more natural it will sound to you.

- Try to develop a rule for everything. A rule is a broad and basic truth. After you get the understanding, give catchy rules to help your child to remember.

- One rule: To find a proper noun, ask yourself "Can I point to that person, or can I find it on a map?" Also, is it a month, day of the week or holiday?

- If they're having difficulty by confusing the noun with the verb, have them ask themselves "Can I do this activity?" If you can, it is not a noun, it's a verb.

- In geography some children get confused with latitude and longitude. For <u>lat</u>itude, remember flat—lie flat. For <u>long</u>itude, remember long—upright.

- In doing graphs on a test always stop first to write in the numbers directly on the graph. Then answer the questions pertaining to the graph. On a line graph, put the number at the dot. On a bar graph, put the number at the top of each bar. The questions are much easier to answer now.

- In doing a math test with many problems of addition and subtraction mixed in, they sometimes get caught up in adding if the last 3 problems were addition and forget to

subtract on the next problem. You can tell your child to first look at the sign, then say to himself "Subtract, subtract I must subtract."

- In doing math homework, first look back on the samples to refresh your memory. Once you understand the samples, then you can proceed with the assigned homework.

- Rounding off to the nearest whole number seems to be a problem initially for small children.

First put a line under the place you're asked to round off to. For example: 7 6, 3̲ 8 4. Round to the nearest hundred. Put a line under the 3 and a bent arrow pointing to the 8. The number the arrow points to is the commander. It tells the 3 to either go up one or stay the same. Five or more it goes up one. Therefore the 3 is now a 4 and every place after the four has a zero. Any number before the 3 remains the same. The problem 76,3̲84 rounded to the nearest hundred is: 76,400.

- In answering homework questions on the chapter you read, underline the key words then look back in the reading to find the sentences surrounding the key words. By paying attention to what you've read, you'll have a quick idea where to look.

- It's often very confusing in English to use the correct pronoun in a sentence. For example, "It was (she, her) who painted that picture." We usually just read it a few times and see which pronoun 'sounds' like it should fit. There's a rule I formulated that gives you the right answer 95% of the time.

1) Distinguish if you have a subject pronoun or object pronoun. Subject pronouns are: I, you, he, she, we, it, they. Object pronouns are: Me, us, him, you, them, it, her.

2) To know if it's a subject pronoun (SP) or an object pronoun (OP), memorize this formula:

SP _____ verb OP TO _____

When you see the word TO in the sentence, the choice is from the set of object pronouns, i.e., Please give these books TO (she, her). To find the SP, first locate the verb and the SP can fit in before it, i.e., Was it (he, him) who won the trophy? Say:? verb ____won HE won.

You wouldn't select HIM because it is an object pronoun and there is no TO word in this sentence.

3) The easy way to know whether the pronoun belongs in the OP or SP category is to say to yourself: Object: TO me, TO her, TO them, TO it, TO you, etc.

Subject: Pick any verb and say: I RAN, she RAN, they RAN, he RAN, etc..

13

BETTER HANDWRITING

In this modern age of telecommunications, some children see writing as a primitive art. You can justify the need for learning to write and to write legibly by showing them how it is a practical part of their lives.

- *Share your own writing with your children.*

- *Show them letters you write to family, businesses, letters received from overseas, etc.*

- *Set up a chalkboard for all family members to communicate in writing phone messages, where they will be, a to-do list, shopping list, etc.*

- *Have them practice good writing and penmanship by writing thank-you letters for gifts they receive, letters to relatives, letters to the editor, letters to their favorite singing group, letters for information on special interests or hobbies, etc.*

Your child needs to know how important it is to have good handwriting in order to be interpreted correctly.

- *Review with them how major errors can be made due to poor handwriting.*

- *Get a good penmanship book from your library, or purchase one in a school supply store (one with traceable, erasable, plastic pages).*

- *If they do a daily journal it should be written neatly and not just scribbled because it's only for mom and not for the teacher.*

- *If your child writes in their journal sloppily and you know they can write neater, let them calmly know that they need to write four more lines for penmanship practice.*

Children should learn very early to take pride in all the work they do and to always present their very best. No sloppy homework should be allowed to be handed in to any teacher.

14

HOW TO MEMORIZE EFFECTIVELY

Memorization is a vital part of academics from kindergarten through college. In knowing the secrets of memorization alone, most children's grades would improve. Some secrets are:

- Read the assignment aloud as if you were sharing it with someone. That helps you to remember it.

- Review what you've learned often. As your child gets into higher grades, have them read their notes just once over from the first day, everyday until the exam.

- Condense your notes into short word phrases so that each phrase represents a lot more information. This would help the visual learner and would be determined by the amount of notes and age of the child. For example, your child has to memorize that archaeologists are people who study ancient times by finding the remains of cities, tombs, etc. They would condense that to: archaeologists = study, ancient, tombs.

- Use memory aids like acronyms for memorizing facts. For example, for the 7 continents remember A A A A A A E. The seven continents are: Asia, Africa, Antarctica, Australia, America (North), America (South), and Europe.

- If you have a list of words to memorize, take the first letter of each word and juggle them about to form a phrase or another word, or a silly saying. Some examples are: To remember the four states that are smaller than New Jersey, you take the first letter of each state and form a word or phrase. D. RICH. The phrase "D RICH man" is easy to remember for Delaware, Rhode Island, Connecticut, and Hawaii. To remember the names of the larger natural lakes in the Highlands of New Jersey: Green Pond and Lake Hopatcong, you can make up a silly phrase. "A Green frog Hops on the pond."

- Question yourself about things in the text you don't comprehend and then summarize important sections.

- Apply what you've learned in math by trying a few extra examples on your own.

- In memorizing written texts like social studies, history, visualize what's taking place like on a movie screen. For example, see the men in combat in the Civil War, half in snow boots and half in shorts with shirts having nos. 1861 and 1865, then add in the general and other important facts you need to remember. This will help you to remember that the Civil War was from 1861–1865 and the North and the South (snow boots and shorts) battled.

- As they do their reading assignment, let them tape themselves with the tape recorder. Continue on the same tape the next day until the chapter is completed. Add expression and creativity as you read with sound effects.

- Play the tape in the morning while dressing for school and at nights while preparing for bed. Kids love to hear themselves, especially if they make it funny.

15

SPELLING MADE EASY

There's no way around it, every child gets spelling words to memorize. In order to make it much easier, identify the learning style of your child and incorporate these secrets. If your child is an auditory learner, he/she may enjoy reading out loud or talking to themselves to help them remember.

- Have them tape record their spelling words to rhythmic music.

When they were younger, my kids had an electric toy microphone with several continuous beats, or they used the electric piano with a rap beat to record their spelling words.

- Have your child pretend he/she is the teacher giving the class an oral spelling test, pausing for each word while it is being taped. Now he can play back the tape any time and use scrap paper to give himself his own spelling test. They even get to grade themselves with the textbook, freeing you up to do other things.

- Take the cassette tape in the car with you and your child can memorize words as they travel.

If your child is more of a visual learner, he can also:

- Write each word on a flash card (cut up cereal boxes) and he can memorize better using his cards.

- Have him largely print the words on paper and place it on the wall by his bed to see as he's dressing in the mornings and at bedtime.

- As you memorize spelling words, break them up into syllables, using phonics.

- For difficult or tricky words, circle the part of the word that trips you up, and convert it into a picture. For example, if the word paranoia gives you trouble and you for-

get if it's *oi* or *io*, think of *oi* words and make a picture of one of them. *Some suggestions: boil, oil, foil, coin. Now you visualize a parachute landing in a pool of black oil. The parachute is to remember PARA and oil is to remember NOIA.*

- *Have them use the new spelling words in speaking and writing.*

- *Tack the words up on the refrigerator and, as you cook, ask them how was their day in school using as many as possible of the spelling words. Or have them tell you a make-believe story using the words.*

16

TELLING TIME

If you have small children, sooner or later they will have to learn how to tell time. To prepare them for this skill, they need to know how to count to 60 by 5's, know their direction of right and left, differentiate between long and short, and understand what is one less than. Many children have difficulty when the hour extends beyond thirty minutes, i.e. 4:45 PM. To help them you can teach them this simple game called "Where is Mr. Long?" Mr. Long is the long hand of the clock. If Mr. Long (the long hand) is to the Left of 12, then the hour is one Less. (Long-Left-Less). For example, if the short hand points to the 3, and Mr. Long is on the left of 12 pointing to the 10, then the hour is one less than 3–2. The hour is 2 and the minutes are 50. To get the minutes you count by fives starting from the 1 on the clock until you get to where Mr. Long is pointing. If Mr. Long is to the Right of 12, then the hour is Right where the short hand points. (Long-Right-Right). For example, if the short hand points to the 3, and Mr. Long is on the right of 12 pointing to the 4, then the hour is right where the short hand points to 3 and the minutes are 20. To get the minutes, you count by fives, starting from the 1 on the clock until you get to where Mr. Long is pointing.

- For practice, buy them a watch with a minute and second hand, not LED (though they are cheaper).

- Hang a kitchen clock with a minute and second hand and while you are cooking you can quiz them on telling time.

- They can even check themselves with your LED wrist watch as long as both clock and watch is synchronized.

- For more practice, draw abut 10 clocks on blank paper but do not draw in the hands. Xerox a few pages of this then fill in the hands of one sheet only and have your child write in the time below.

- *Remind him/her that the first thing to do is ask: "Where is Mr. Long?"*

- *Everywhere you go (stores, church, bank, etc.) and see a clock, ask your child to tell you the time.*

17

LEARNING ABOUT MONEY

Children need to know how to identify coins and bills, the value of money, its use, and how to get change.

- *Have them identify coins whenever you can—shopping, at the bank, paying tolls, etc.*

- *In the store let them pay the cashier when purchasing items and have them count the change.*

- *You can tape front and back of coins and bills to blank paper, without writing in the value, then xerox 2 or 3 copies.*

- *Hang a copy in their room, writing in each value below the coin or bill.*

- *Keep another copy on the refrigerator so while you're cooking they can review with you.*

- *Teach them that learning to add money is the same as adding numerals.*

- *With a deck of cards and play money or real money, play with them and their siblings or friends, <u>The Money Game</u>. Using 2 or more players, deal 5–10 cards to each player from the deck. Each player has pencil and paper. Place some money on the table and each one writes down the amount. If they are correct, they discard a card, if they're wrong, they pick up a card from the deck. The first one to discard all cards wins.*

- *Using play money while you're cooking or doing laundry, take out the supermarket flyer and let them show you the amount of the item in coins and bills. You can also teach them making change using the same flyer.*

- Another fun way to help them learn about money is to use play money and have them purchase their meals, especially their desserts from you.

18

LEARNING A NEW LANGUAGE

As your child advances in school, they usually are required to learn a foreign language. Before they can master another language, they first must know English grammar. They need to know the basic function and definition of nouns, verbs, pronouns, adjectives, etc.

- If you own a computer, I suggest getting an inexpensive teaching language game for your computer. Most kids are drawn to the computer, so they can learn as they play.

- If you don't own a computer, you can reserve time at the library's computer. If they don't have a language disc., ask if you can buy your own and bring it there to use.

- Have them review their vocabulary words on cassette tape. If their pronunciation is bad and you don't have a clue, ask a friend that knows the language to say the words for you in the tape recorder. This can even be done over the telephone.

- Teach them to always translate from English into the other language and not the other way around.

- The easiest way to learn a foreign vocabulary quickly and to memorize the pronunciation is to make a chart listing:

English Spanish Pronunciation Memory Aid.

- The Memory Aid is a silly sentence comprised of the pronunciation and the English word. For example, to memorize in Spanish the word for city (la ciudad), remember the sentence: See you dad, in the city.

- Another example, to memorize in Spanish the word for brother (el hermano), remember the memory aid sentence: Oh brother, don't touch her man. The French

word for bank is banque (pronounced bahnk). Use the pronunciation and the English to make a silly sentence: Bobby went <u>bonk</u>ers at the <u>bank.</u>

- Once you know some basic vocabulary, memorizing idioms can be more productive than learning single words.

- As they become more advanced and are assigned passages to read, first skim the passage to get a sense of what it is about. Then go back to grasp the vocabulary and grammar within the context of the whole passage.

19

READ TO AND WITH YOUR CHILD

I strongly believe that good reading ability is the foundation for a successful education. A child can never be too young to be read to. Reading to your child is a habit that should start when they are newborns and continue. Reading aloud to children of all ages helps them to develop an imagination and a love for books.

- Quality of time spent together is more important than quantity of time. Your child will remember ten minutes of reading together far longer than three hours of TV.

- Don't read stories you don't really enjoy. It will show in your reading. If you're very busy and started a good mystery book, kill two birds with one stone and read it to your older kids with expression. This will cause them to visualize well and enable them to comprehend, and you get to finish your book.

- For younger children, choose a book together and take turns reading. Your child might be focusing on how to read and reading in between helps to keep the story alive.

- Don't be surprised if your young child interrupts with a lot of questions. You should answer the question right away and move on.

- Use this reading time to help your child learn visualization, verbalization, and comprehension from a very early age. (See the previous chapter Basic Overview—Comprehension Disorder.)

- In addition to reading, you should also practice story telling. Reminisce about when you were their age, special events with your parents, brothers, or sisters.

- Remember to use a lot of adjectives, giving much graphic description to stir their imagination

- *Have them tell you stories about what happened on special occasions, a funny story from school, etc. You then ask what they were wearing, how tall was the teacher, what time of day, the setting, etc. to help them better visualize and to verbalize their story.*

- *Once they've verbalized their story, have them write about it including all the adjectives, etc. If they're too young to write about it, you should write it for them.*

- *You can subscribe to a children's magazine that has characters they know from TV that they can relate to. Youngsters usually get pleasure from receiving their own mail.*

- *You need to set the example for your children and let them see you reading.*

- *Encourage your children to read by introducing them to the public library at an early age. Have them experience the importance of having their own library card.*

20

MAKING SAMPLE TESTS

Making up sample tests helps your child to remember the material and prepares them for the test to be given in school. It causes them to learn how to focus their minds on the most important materials. At first when they were younger, I made up the tests for my kids. By the time they reached the fifth grade they were formulating their own sample tests. Now all I have to do is say to them, "Go use your textbook and notes and make up a sample test." At first when they started on their own, I would glance through it and show them important points they left out. Now they've been doing it so long that I don't have to check the sample test, only let them know it's their responsibility.

- Go through the chapter as the first assignment is given and make up a sample test using the words in bold print and the chapter review information.

- Use a carbon paper beneath and circle the right answers as you go along.

- Use the same format that his/her teacher would use, i.e., multiple choice, matching, true/false, diagram.

- Don't allow your child to write the answers on the original so you can administer the test a few times for the week.

- Put the chapter, title, grade, and year the sample test was written. If you have younger children who will be passing through these grades, save these tests.

- If your child has many facts to remember, make up a matching column test to help him/her identify <u>key</u> <u>words</u>, no matter how the sentence is phrased, they'll recognize those words and remember the information associated with them and be better able to answer the question.

- Pay special attention to handouts with drawings or book illustrations. They may appear unlabeled on a school test.

- Trace two copies of these diagrams and labels using tracing paper. Fill in the answers on one copy for yourself and have them write their answers on a separate scrap paper.

- You can have them take their own test and correct themselves. This is when your early labor in younger years pays off.

- To now solidify this knowledge, they must now fold the matching column paper in half and be able to read the information in column B and relate the information to column A.

- If your child can do both sides of their matching column, answer the questions at the end of each section and correctly do the chapter review, then they should pass the exam with a good grade.

- With these study skills being reinforced in middle school, studying in high school and college will be easier as they become more independent.

- Remember: Its Never Too Late To Start!

21

ORGANIZING NOTES

As your child reaches middle school and above, they will have to learn how to listen in class and take notes. A lot of what the teacher says in class will be on the exam. Good note-taking becomes more critical as they grow older.

- Come prepared for class by reading ahead on what will be covered in class. Listen 80% of the time and write 20% of the time.

- Keep your notes neat, arranging main ideas under headings using outline form.

- Use shorthand and abbreviations when possible: w/with w/o without info. information govt government R right L left ^ increase

- Record the main ideas and use your own words, not the teacher's.

- Record any information your teacher repeats more than once, or deems important enough to write it on the blackboard.

- Listen well for clues your teacher drops, indicating that the following information is very important.

- Some clues are: "The main theme is…", "What's important for you to know is…", "A major development was…", "Take note of…", "We can then conclude that…"

- On occasion, compare notes of your close classmates to see who is good at note-taking just in case you do miss a class and will definitely need to borrow notes.

22

LEARNING MULTIPLICATION

The time will come when your child has to learn the multiplication table. It begins with rote memory and later becomes a part of them. To help your child know multiplication with speed, use carbon paper and write about seven rows of the tables. Cut each row into strips. Have them complete each strip with greater speed. The goal is to complete a strip in 30 seconds.

- Use a sand clock if you have one and your child can practice on his own, freeing you up for other things.

- A secret for learning the 9 x tables is, the answer is always one less than the number multiplied, and the second number added to that always equals 9. For example, 9 x 8 = 72. One less than 8 is 7. The number added to 7 that equals 9 is 2. (7 + 2 = 9). 9 x 4 = 36. One less than 4 is 3. (3 + ? = 9).

- You can teach them that 10 x any number can be found by adding a zero to that number.

- Multiplying by 11 is simply writing the number twice and you'll get your answer.

23

TEACHING BASIC TYPING

We are now in the age of computers where children are learning how to use computers in preschool and kindergarten classrooms. Many can play computer games, create designs, know how to use the internet but are not able to type. I believe they should know the basics of using a keyboard correctly so that later on they will be able to type their own book reports without using one and two fingers only.

- Start by getting a basic typing book from your library and have them to practice a few minutes a day.

- You can purchase an inexpensive typing computer game that would be more exciting to them while challenging them to reach different levels.

- Once they have learned the keyboard, have them type their spelling words (accomplishing two tasks at once.)

- As they become older, have them practice their writing skills by creating stories on the computer by typing and not looking at the keyboard.

24

WRITING A BOOK REPORT

Book reports can be written in different ways. Sometimes the teacher gives a hand-out with a sample of how it is to be done. If there is no guideline, kids can waste so much time trying to decide how to write the book report. Having an outline before they start helps them to cluster related pieces of information. A suggested outline for a fictional book report is as follows:

Title:

Author:

Illustrator:

I. Brief overview about the book. The story is about…

II. Who are the characters involved in the action, naming the main character first?

III. Where and when does the action take place?

IV. Elaborate on the story without revealing the ending. Leave the reader at an interesting part near the end, suggesting they read the book to find out the ending.

V. Conclusion. Did you like the book? Why or why not?

A suggested outline for a non-fictional book report is as follows:

Title:

Author:

Illustrator:

I. What is the subject of this book? Give highlights of the book in detail.

II. How does the author make the subject interesting?

III. How do you feel while reading this book?

IV. Would you suggest this book to a friend? Why or why not?

Remember to have them proofread all work first and reinforce completing sentences or thoughts. Having them to read the report out loud helps in identifying incomplete sentences and thoughts. Make sure the tenses (past and present) are in agreement in each sentence.

25

WRITING A TERM PAPER

As your children reach the upper grades they will be challenged with writing term papers. The key to a good term paper is knowing your topic and following an outline. If the teacher gives a series of topics to choose from, select the topic that most interests you. If undecided, find some short periodicals in the library on the topics that cover most of the information in them. You can then choose the one that is most extensive with facts. Next you re-read this article for better understanding of the topic. From here you make up an outline. A sample outline would be:

TOPIC:_____

INTRODUCTION:_____

1._____

2._____

I._____

A._____

1._____

2._____

B._____

1._____

2._____

II._____

A._____

1._____

2._____

B._____

1._____

2._____

CONCLUSION:_____

As you take the most salient points to formulate your outline, you then look for other articles/books that expound on just those points in the author's writing. With computers in libraries you can zero in on very specific information for each category. To begin with, you will read the introduction of your first article and choose two or three other good articles or books. Combine their introductions along with your thoughts to form a comprehensive introduction. Remember, you are not copying the words of the authors. That is called plagiarism. For each point you will combine the viewpoint of each author along with your thoughts to formulate a paragraph. Continue until you wrap up with your conclusion. Having this outline will keep your thoughts organized and your term paper more focused.

26

TEST TAKING SKILLS

- *Avoid cramming by studying daily way in advance using your sample tests.*

- *Don't be anxious! If you know you prepared well with the chapter review, matching column tests, knowing diagrams, spelling words, etc. chances are you'll do well.*

- *Be on time for the test and have all the tools you'll need to complete the test.*

- *First listen carefully to the teacher's instructions. Find out if you will be penalized for wrong answers. If you won't be penalized then guess answers you're not sure of. In this case, don't leave any questions blank.*

- *Read all directions twice, then go back and underline key words.*

- *Do the easiest most valuable questions first to boost your confidence.*

- *Put a check next to the questions you did not answer.*

- *Sometimes other questions on the test will help provide the answer for you.*

- *Answer a multiple choice question first in your head and then look for the answer that closely matches it.*

- *Always proofread your test before handing it in. Reread the directions one last time.*

27

MAKING A SUMMER CALENDAR

Kids and parents alike look forward to summer because of no homework. Sadly enough many kids do nothing but play all summer and return to school in the fall and have forgotten everything. Teachers usually spend the first month of school just reviewing what was taught last year. Remember, whatever you don't use you will lose. You can set up a summer calendar for your kids to keep their minds refreshed and make it easier on both of you when school begins. Depending on the age, many children have to read at least one book and do a report or a project on that book. Have your child read one or two chapters a day and write a brief summary of that chapter. This writing helps them to practice good writing skills and to remember the entire story when it's time for the report. Before beginning the next chapter, they need to read their previous notes. Designate a day for completion, allowing for trips and unexpected events. At the end the book report is written. On the calendar should be certain days set aside for instrument practice. They should practice their scales and various songs at least for a half hour.

Before school was let out, if you had copied pages of their math book at the Section Review, you can now assign a page to be done on certain days of the week.

Children who need more practice in writing can be given fun topics to choose from to write about one or two days in the week:

- *If I Spent The Weekend With Britney Spears!*

- *What I Could Teach Michael Jordan About Basketball!*

- *The Best and Worst Stores In The Mall!*

- What Boys Should Know About Dressing!

Part of their summer calendar can be 30 minutes on the computer learning a foreign language they'll be getting in school or learning to type.

Some summer reading incentives for your kids for completing books can be small gifts, McDonald's treat, small amount of money, video game rentals, a movie, etc. Getting them to read and to like reading is worth the money spent.

28

PRAYING FOR YOUR CHILDREN

This book came out from my struggles, trials, failures, and successes with my own children. At times it was very challenging especially not being able to understand how I could better help them to comprehend. The teachers had told me that my child did have a learning problem and would find schoolwork challenging, but no one told me exactly what I could do. I sought the Lord concerning this and He gave me guidance on how to incorporate all these ideas into helping them learn. I truly believe that if I were not in constant prayer to the Lord, my child would have poor self-esteem and would have been held back many times. A dear friend once told me, "The degree to which you will minister to others, is the degree to which you will be tested."

It is so vitally important to realize that our children are gifts from God. They are uniquely and wonderfully made and their Designer knows them the best. As wise parents we should seek the Designer, the Creator of our children as to how to best bring out in them what He has put there in seed form. Any wise person would refer to the owner's manual in trying to learn how to operate an unfamiliar item they possess. We discover new things and new ways about our children daily. I strongly believe our owner's manual is the Holy Bible and it should be read daily. Being in direct communication with the Designer/Creator is done through daily prayer. You need to pray God's protection over each child at all times, pray for understanding, an open mind to receive instruction in school, pray for wisdom—the application of knowledge, and pray for a sound healthy mind in your child.

There are promises God has given us that we need to rehearse daily. The Bible tells us to "hold fast the profession of our faith without wavering; for He is faithful that promised;" KJV (Heb. 10:23). As parents we need to be consistent, not giving up easily or becoming discouraged. "The Lord is not slack concerning his promise, as some men count slackness; but is longsuffering to usward,. KJV (2 Peter 3:9). Jesus tells us in John 15:7, "If you abide in Me, and My words abide in you, you will ask what you desire, and it shall be done for you." KJV.

APPENDIX

SUGGESTED READING

Cheryl R. Carter. Organizing Your Home, A Practical Guide For Bringing Peace And Order To Your Home, (Jehonadah Communications, Uniondale, New York, 1999).

Cheryl R. Carter. Organize Your Life! A Comprehensive Guide To Time Management, Goal Setting And Productivity Just For Women, (Jehonadah Communications, Uniondale, New York, 1999).

Dr. James C. Dobson. Parenting Isn't For Cowards, (Word Publishing, Dallas, 1987).

Beverly LaHaye. How To Develop Your Child's Temperament, (Harvest House Publishers, Eugene, Oregon, 1977).

Jamie Buckingham. Power For Living, (Arthur S. DeMoss Foundation, 1988).

Nanci Bell. Visualizing and Verbalizing For Language Comprehension And Thinking, (Academy of Reading Publications, Pasa Robles, Calif., 1991).

Cynthia Ulrich Tobias. The Way They Learn, (Focus On The Family Publishing, Colorado Springs, CO, 1994).

About the Author

Joan Brown has always been a scholastic achiever. She graduated cum laude from Hunter College with a Bachelor's of Science in Nursing. She also graduated cum laude with a Master's degree from Columbia University, and was valedictorian of her high school. Her love for teaching was first ignited when she tutored students for the New York City Board of Education. She has tutored many children and adults in academics and nursing over the years.

Using the techniques in this book she moved her daughter from basic skills classes to achieve induction into the National Honor Society. She's certain that any parent can do the same using the techniques in this book.

She works full-time and is married, with two children. Currently she resides in Colonia, New Jersey.

0-595-29502-9